THIS JOURNAL BELONGS TO:

....

WELL-READ WOMEN

—— A READER'S JOURNAL ——

by Samantha Hahn

CHRONICLE BOOKS

SAN FRANCISCO

ISBN: 978-1-4521-4302-6

Manufactured in China.

Design by Kristen Hewitt

10 9 8 7 6 5 4 3 2 1

Chronicle Books LLC
680 Second Street
San Francisco, CA 94107
www.chroniclebooks.com

A READER'S JOURNAL

The greatest characters inflame our passions and excite our imaginations. They linger in our minds long after we've read the last line on the last page. Our favorite characters are universal archetypes and uniquely flawed individuals all at once. Their stories stay with us. We sympathize with them; we admire them; we hate them; we want to be them. And we never want to forget them.

Use this reader's journal as a place to collect all your impressions and memories. The Book Notes pages allow you to log each book you read with some notes about the plots and characters, and offer room to jot down notable quotations so you never forget what you loved (or hated!) about each book. Keep a running list of what you want to read next in the Books to Check Out section. There are blank notes pages to hold general thoughts that don't pertain to a specific title. And at the back, in the Reading Inspiration section, are lists of prizewinning books—plus room for you to create a list of your own personal prize-worthy reads.

So many books await. Enjoy them.

BOOK
NOTES

DATE STARTED

___ / ___ / ___

DATE FINISHED

___ / ___ / ___

RATE THIS BOOK

1 2 3 4 5

BOOK TITLE: _____

_____

AUTHOR: _____

_____

PLOT NOTES: _____

_____

_____

_____

_____

_____

_____

_____

CHARACTER NOTES: _____

_____

_____

_____

_____

_____

FAVORITE QUOTES: _____

_____

_____

_____

_____

_____

OTHER BOOKS TO READ BY THIS AUTHOR: _____

_____

BOOK TITLE: _____

_____

AUTHOR: _____

_____

PLOT NOTES: _____

_____

_____

_____

_____

_____

_____

_____

CHARACTER NOTES: _____

_____

_____

_____

_____

_____

FAVORITE QUOTES: _____

_____

_____

_____

_____

_____

OTHER BOOKS TO READ BY THIS AUTHOR: _____

_____

DATE STARTED

___ / ___ / ___

DATE FINISHED

___ / ___ / ___

RATE THIS BOOK

1   2   3   4   5

DATE STARTED

—— / —— / ——

DATE FINISHED

—— / —— / ——

RATE THIS BOOK

1   2   3   4   5

BOOK TITLE: _____

_____

AUTHOR: _____

_____

PLOT NOTES: _____

_____

_____

_____

_____

_____

_____

CHARACTER NOTES: _____

_____

_____

_____

_____

_____

FAVORITE QUOTES: _____

_____

_____

_____

_____

_____

OTHER BOOKS TO READ BY THIS AUTHOR: _____

_____

BOOK TITLE: _____

_____

AUTHOR: _____

_____

PLOT NOTES: _____

_____

_____

_____

_____

_____

_____

CHARACTER NOTES: _____

_____

_____

_____

_____

FAVORITE QUOTES: _____

_____

_____

_____

_____

OTHER BOOKS TO READ BY THIS AUTHOR: _____

_____

DATE STARTED

___ / ___ / ___

DATE FINISHED

___ / ___ / ___

RATE THIS BOOK

1   2   3   4   5

A lady's imagination is very
rapid; it jumps from admiration to love,
from love to matrimony in a moment.

ELIZABETH BENNET

Pride and Prejudice by Jane Austen

DATE STARTED

___ / ___ / ___

DATE FINISHED

___ / ___ / ___

RATE THIS BOOK

1   2   3   4   5

BOOK TITLE: _____

_____

AUTHOR: _____

_____

PLOT NOTES: _____

_____

_____

_____

_____

_____

CHARACTER NOTES: _____

_____

_____

_____

_____

_____

FAVORITE QUOTES: _____

_____

_____

_____

_____

_____

OTHER BOOKS TO READ BY THIS AUTHOR: _____

_____

BOOK TITLE: _____

_____

AUTHOR: _____

_____

PLOT NOTES: _____

_____

_____

_____

_____

_____

_____

CHARACTER NOTES: _____

_____

_____

_____

_____

_____

FAVORITE QUOTES: _____

_____

_____

_____

_____

_____

OTHER BOOKS TO READ BY THIS AUTHOR: _____

_____

DATE STARTED

—— / —— / ——

DATE FINISHED

—— / —— / ——

RATE THIS BOOK

1   2   3   4   5

DATE STARTED

—— / —— / ——

DATE FINISHED

—— / —— / ——

RATE THIS BOOK

1   2   3   4   5

BOOK TITLE: _____

_____

AUTHOR: _____

_____

PLOT NOTES: _____

_____

_____

_____

_____

_____

_____

CHARACTER NOTES: _____

_____

_____

_____

_____

_____

FAVORITE QUOTES: _____

_____

_____

_____

_____

_____

OTHER BOOKS TO READ BY THIS AUTHOR: _____

_____

BOOK TITLE: _____

_____

AUTHOR: _____

_____

PLOT NOTES: _____

_____

_____

_____

_____

_____

CHARACTER NOTES: _____

_____

_____

_____

_____

_____

FAVORITE QUOTES: _____

_____

_____

_____

_____

OTHER BOOKS TO READ BY THIS AUTHOR: _____

_____

DATE STARTED

___ / ___ / ___

DATE FINISHED

___ / ___ / ___

RATE THIS BOOK

1   2   3   4   5

Haven't I striven,
striven with all my strength,
to find something
to give meaning to my life?

ANNA KARENINA
Anna Karenina by Leo Tolstoy

DATE STARTED

—— / —— / ——

DATE FINISHED

—— / —— / ——

RATE THIS BOOK

1   2   3   4   5

BOOK TITLE: _____

_____

AUTHOR: _____

_____

PLOT NOTES: _____

_____

_____

_____

_____

_____

_____

_____

CHARACTER NOTES: _____

_____

_____

_____

_____

_____

FAVORITE QUOTES: _____

_____

_____

_____

_____

_____

OTHER BOOKS TO READ BY THIS AUTHOR: _____

_____

BOOK TITLE: _____

_____

AUTHOR: _____

_____

PLOT NOTES: _____

_____

_____

_____

_____

_____

_____

CHARACTER NOTES: _____

_____

_____

_____

_____

_____

FAVORITE QUOTES: _____

_____

_____

_____

_____

OTHER BOOKS TO READ BY THIS AUTHOR: _____

_____

DATE STARTED

—— / —— / ——

DATE FINISHED

—— / —— / ——

RATE THIS BOOK

1   2   3   4   5

BOOK TITLE: _____

_____

AUTHOR: _____

_____

PLOT NOTES: _____

_____

_____

_____

_____

_____

_____

CHARACTER NOTES: _____

_____

_____

_____

_____

_____

FAVORITE QUOTES: _____

_____

_____

_____

_____

_____

OTHER BOOKS TO READ BY THIS AUTHOR: _____

_____

BOOK TITLE: _____

_____

AUTHOR: _____

_____

PLOT NOTES: _____

_____

_____

_____

_____

_____

_____

CHARACTER NOTES: _____

_____

_____

_____

_____

_____

FAVORITE QUOTES: _____

_____

_____

_____

_____

_____

OTHER BOOKS TO READ BY THIS AUTHOR: _____

_____

DATE STARTED

___ / ___ / ___

DATE FINISHED

___ / ___ / ___

RATE THIS BOOK

1   2   3   4   5

Laws and principles

are not for the times

when there is no temptation. . .

JANE EYRE

Jane Eyre by Charlotte Brontë

DATE STARTED

—— / —— / ——

DATE FINISHED

—— / —— / ——

RATE THIS BOOK

1   2   3   4   5

BOOK TITLE: _____

_____

AUTHOR: _____

_____

PLOT NOTES: _____

_____

_____

_____

_____

_____

_____

CHARACTER NOTES: _____

_____

_____

_____

_____

FAVORITE QUOTES: _____

_____

_____

_____

_____

OTHER BOOKS TO READ BY THIS AUTHOR: _____

_____

BOOK TITLE: _____

_____

AUTHOR: _____

_____

PLOT NOTES: _____

_____

_____

_____

_____

_____

_____

CHARACTER NOTES: _____

_____

_____

_____

_____

_____

FAVORITE QUOTES: _____

_____

_____

_____

_____

_____

OTHER BOOKS TO READ BY THIS AUTHOR: _____

_____

DATE STARTED

__ / __ / __

DATE FINISHED

__ / __ / __

RATE THIS BOOK

1   2   3   4   5

DATE STARTED

—— / —— / ——

DATE FINISHED

—— / —— / ——

RATE THIS BOOK

1   2   3   4   5

BOOK TITLE: _____

_____

AUTHOR: _____

_____

PLOT NOTES: _____

_____

_____

_____

_____

_____

_____

CHARACTER NOTES: _____

_____

_____

_____

_____

_____

FAVORITE QUOTES: _____

_____

_____

_____

_____

_____

OTHER BOOKS TO READ BY THIS AUTHOR: _____

_____

BOOK TITLE: _____

_____

AUTHOR: _____

_____

PLOT NOTES: _____

_____

_____

_____

_____

_____

_____

CHARACTER NOTES: _____

_____

_____

_____

_____

_____

FAVORITE QUOTES: _____

_____

_____

_____

_____

OTHER BOOKS TO READ BY THIS AUTHOR: _____

_____

DATE STARTED

___ / ___ / ___

DATE FINISHED

___ / ___ / ___

RATE THIS BOOK

1   2   3   4   5

It seems as if I could do anything
when I'm in a passion.
I get so savage, I could hurt anyone
and enjoy it.

JO MARCH
Little Women by Louisa May Alcott

DATE STARTED

___ / ___ / ___

DATE FINISHED

___ / ___ / ___

RATE THIS BOOK

1   2   3   4   5

BOOK TITLE: _____

_____

AUTHOR: _____

_____

PLOT NOTES: _____

_____

_____

_____

_____

_____

_____

CHARACTER NOTES: _____

_____

_____

_____

_____

_____

FAVORITE QUOTES: _____

_____

_____

_____

_____

_____

OTHER BOOKS TO READ BY THIS AUTHOR: _____

_____

BOOK TITLE: _____

_____

AUTHOR: _____

_____

PLOT NOTES: _____

_____

_____

_____

_____

_____

_____

_____

CHARACTER NOTES: _____

_____

_____

_____

_____

_____

FAVORITE QUOTES: _____

_____

_____

_____

_____

_____

OTHER BOOKS TO READ BY THIS AUTHOR: _____

_____

DATE STARTED

___ / ___ / ___

DATE FINISHED

___ / ___ / ___

RATE THIS BOOK

1 2 3 4 5

DATE STARTED

___ / ___ / ___

DATE FINISHED

___ / ___ / ___

RATE THIS BOOK

1   2   3   4   5

BOOK TITLE: _____

_____

AUTHOR: _____

_____

PLOT NOTES: _____

_____

_____

_____

_____

_____

_____

CHARACTER NOTES: _____

_____

_____

_____

_____

_____

FAVORITE QUOTES: _____

_____

_____

_____

_____

_____

OTHER BOOKS TO READ BY THIS AUTHOR: _____

_____

BOOK TITLE: _____

_____

AUTHOR: _____

_____

PLOT NOTES: _____

_____

_____

_____

_____

_____

_____

CHARACTER NOTES: _____

_____

_____

_____

_____

_____

FAVORITE QUOTES: _____

_____

_____

_____

_____

_____

OTHER BOOKS TO READ BY THIS AUTHOR: _____

_____

DATE STARTED

___ / ___ / ___

DATE FINISHED

___ / ___ / ___

RATE THIS BOOK

1   2   3   4   5

If you knew how great is a mother's love...you would have no fear.

WENDY DARLING

Peter Pan by J.M. Barrie

DATE STARTED

___ / ___ / ___

DATE FINISHED

___ / ___ / ___

RATE THIS BOOK

1   2   3   4   5

BOOK TITLE: _____

_____

AUTHOR: _____

_____

PLOT NOTES: _____

_____

_____

_____

_____

_____

_____

_____

CHARACTER NOTES: _____

_____

_____

_____

_____

_____

FAVORITE QUOTES: _____

_____

_____

_____

_____

_____

OTHER BOOKS TO READ BY THIS AUTHOR: _____

_____

BOOK TITLE: _____

AUTHOR: _____

PLOT NOTES: _____
_____
_____
_____
_____
_____
_____

CHARACTER NOTES: _____
_____
_____
_____
_____
_____

FAVORITE QUOTES: _____
_____
_____
_____
_____
_____

OTHER BOOKS TO READ BY THIS AUTHOR: _____
_____

DATE STARTED

—— / —— / ——

DATE FINISHED

—— / —— / ——

RATE THIS BOOK

1   2   3   4   5

DATE STARTED

—— / —— / ——

DATE FINISHED

—— / —— / ——

RATE THIS BOOK

1   2   3   4   5

BOOK TITLE: _____

_____

AUTHOR: _____

_____

PLOT NOTES: _____

_____

_____

_____

_____

_____

_____

_____

CHARACTER NOTES: _____

_____

_____

_____

_____

_____

FAVORITE QUOTES: _____

_____

_____

_____

_____

_____

OTHER BOOKS TO READ BY THIS AUTHOR: _____

_____

BOOK TITLE: _____

AUTHOR: _____

PLOT NOTES: _____
_____
_____
_____
_____
_____
_____
_____

CHARACTER NOTES: _____
_____
_____
_____
_____
_____

FAVORITE QUOTES: _____
_____
_____
_____
_____
_____

OTHER BOOKS TO READ BY THIS AUTHOR: _____
_____

DATE STARTED

___ / ___ / ___

DATE FINISHED

___ / ___ / ___

....

RATE THIS BOOK

1   2   3   4   5

My nature is for mutual love, not hate.

Antigone by Sophocles

DATE STARTED

—— / —— / ——

DATE FINISHED

—— / —— / ——

RATE THIS BOOK

1   2   3   4   5

BOOK TITLE: _____

_____

AUTHOR: _____

_____

PLOT NOTES: _____

_____

_____

_____

_____

_____

_____

CHARACTER NOTES: _____

_____

_____

_____

_____

_____

FAVORITE QUOTES: _____

_____

_____

_____

_____

OTHER BOOKS TO READ BY THIS AUTHOR: ____

_____

BOOK TITLE: _____

_____

AUTHOR: _____

_____

PLOT NOTES: _____

_____

_____

_____

_____

_____

_____

_____

CHARACTER NOTES: _____

_____

_____

_____

_____

_____

_____

FAVORITE QUOTES: _____

_____

_____

_____

_____

_____

OTHER BOOKS TO READ BY THIS AUTHOR: _____

_____

DATE STARTED

___ / ___ / ___

DATE FINISHED

___ / ___ / ___

RATE THIS BOOK

1 2 3 4 5

DATE STARTED

—— / —— / ——

DATE FINISHED

—— / —— / ——

RATE THIS BOOK

1   2   3   4   5

BOOK TITLE: _____

_____

AUTHOR: _____

_____

PLOT NOTES: _____

_____

_____

_____

_____

_____

_____

_____

CHARACTER NOTES: _____

_____

_____

_____

_____

_____

_____

FAVORITE QUOTES: _____

_____

_____

_____

_____

_____

_____

OTHER BOOKS TO READ BY THIS AUTHOR: _____

_____

BOOK TITLE: _____

AUTHOR: _____

PLOT NOTES: _____
_____
_____
_____
_____
_____
_____

CHARACTER NOTES: _____
_____
_____
_____
_____
_____

FAVORITE QUOTES: _____
_____
_____
_____
_____

OTHER BOOKS TO READ BY THIS AUTHOR: _____
_____

DATE STARTED

___ / ___ / ___

DATE FINISHED

___ / ___ / ___

RATE THIS BOOK

1 2 3 4 5

This sensation of listlessness, weariness, stupidity,

this disinclination to sit down

and employ myself,

this feeling of every thing's being dull and insipid about the house!

I must be in love;

I should be the oddest creature in the world

if I were not—

for a few weeks at least.

EMMA WOODHOUSE
Emma by Jane Austen

DATE STARTED

—— / —— / ——

DATE FINISHED

—— / —— / ——

RATE THIS BOOK

1 2 3 4 5

BOOK TITLE: _____

_____

AUTHOR: _____

_____

PLOT NOTES: _____

_____

_____

_____

_____

_____

_____

CHARACTER NOTES: _____

_____

_____

_____

_____

_____

FAVORITE QUOTES: _____

_____

_____

_____

_____

_____

_____

OTHER BOOKS TO READ BY THIS AUTHOR: _____

_____

BOOK TITLE: _____

AUTHOR: _____

PLOT NOTES: _____

_____

_____

_____

_____

_____

_____

CHARACTER NOTES: _____

_____

_____

_____

_____

_____

FAVORITE QUOTES: _____

_____

_____

_____

_____

OTHER BOOKS TO READ BY THIS AUTHOR: _____

_____

DATE STARTED

___ / ___ / ___

DATE FINISHED

___ / ___ / ___

RATE THIS BOOK

1   2   3   4   5

DATE STARTED

—— / —— / ——

DATE FINISHED

—— / —— / ——

RATE THIS BOOK

1   2   3   4   5

BOOK TITLE: _____

_____

AUTHOR: _____

_____

PLOT NOTES: _____

_____

_____

_____

_____

_____

_____

CHARACTER NOTES: _____

_____

_____

_____

_____

_____

FAVORITE QUOTES: _____

_____

_____

_____

_____

_____

OTHER BOOKS TO READ BY THIS AUTHOR: _____

_____

BOOK TITLE: _____

_____

AUTHOR: _____

_____

PLOT NOTES: _____

_____

_____

_____

_____

_____

_____

CHARACTER NOTES: _____

_____

_____

_____

_____

FAVORITE QUOTES: _____

_____

_____

_____

_____

OTHER BOOKS TO READ BY THIS AUTHOR: _____

_____

DATE STARTED

___ / ___ / ___

DATE FINISHED

___ / ___ / ___

RATE THIS BOOK

1 2 3 4 5

My love is deep;
the more I give to thee,
the more I have,
for both are infinite.

JULIET CAPULET

Romeo and Juliet by William Shakespeare

DATE STARTED

—— / —— / ——

DATE FINISHED

—— / —— / ——

RATE THIS BOOK

1   2   3   4   5

BOOK TITLE: _____

_____

AUTHOR: _____

_____

PLOT NOTES: _____

_____

_____

_____

_____

_____

_____

CHARACTER NOTES: _____

_____

_____

_____

_____

_____

FAVORITE QUOTES: _____

_____

_____

_____

_____

OTHER BOOKS TO READ BY THIS AUTHOR: _____

_____

BOOK TITLE: _____

_____

AUTHOR: _____

_____

PLOT NOTES: _____

_____

_____

_____

_____

_____

CHARACTER NOTES: _____

_____

_____

_____

_____

FAVORITE QUOTES: _____

_____

_____

_____

_____

OTHER BOOKS TO READ BY THIS AUTHOR: _____

_____

DATE STARTED

—— / —— / ——

DATE FINISHED

—— / —— / ——

RATE THIS BOOK

1   2   3   4   5

BOOK TITLE: _____

_____

AUTHOR: _____

_____

PLOT NOTES: _____

_____

_____

_____

_____

_____

_____

_____

CHARACTER NOTES: _____

_____

_____

_____

_____

FAVORITE QUOTES: _____

_____

_____

_____

_____

_____

OTHER BOOKS TO READ BY THIS AUTHOR: _____

_____

BOOK TITLE: _____

_____

AUTHOR: _____

_____

PLOT NOTES: _____

_____

_____

_____

_____

_____

_____

CHARACTER NOTES: _____

_____

_____

_____

_____

_____

FAVORITE QUOTES: _____

_____

_____

_____

_____

_____

OTHER BOOKS TO READ BY THIS AUTHOR: _____

_____

DATE STARTED

___ / ___ / ___

DATE FINISHED

___ / ___ / ___

RATE THIS BOOK

1   2   3   4   5

You learn things by saying them over and over

and thinking about them

until they stay in your mind forever.

MARY LENNOX
The Secret Garden by Frances Hodgson Burnett

DATE STARTED

—— / —— / ——

DATE FINISHED

—— / —— / ——

RATE THIS BOOK

1   2   3   4   5

BOOK TITLE: _____

_____

AUTHOR: _____

_____

PLOT NOTES: _____

_____

_____

_____

_____

_____

_____

CHARACTER NOTES: _____

_____

_____

_____

_____

_____

FAVORITE QUOTES: _____

_____

_____

_____

_____

_____

OTHER BOOKS TO READ BY THIS AUTHOR: _____

_____

BOOK TITLE: _____

_____

AUTHOR: _____

_____

PLOT NOTES: _____

_____

_____

_____

_____

_____

_____

CHARACTER NOTES: _____

_____

_____

_____

_____

_____

FAVORITE QUOTES: _____

_____

_____

_____

_____

_____

OTHER BOOKS TO READ BY THIS AUTHOR: _____

_____

DATE STARTED

___ / ___ / ___

DATE FINISHED

___ / ___ / ___

RATE THIS BOOK

1   2   3   4   5

DATE STARTED

____ / ____ / ____

DATE FINISHED

____ / ____ / ____

RATE THIS BOOK

1   2   3   4   5

BOOK TITLE: _____

_____

AUTHOR: _____

_____

PLOT NOTES: _____

_____

_____

_____

_____

CHARACTER NOTES: _____

_____

_____

_____

_____

FAVORITE QUOTES: _____

_____

_____

_____

_____

OTHER BOOKS TO READ BY THIS AUTHOR: _____

_____

BOOK TITLE: _____

_____

AUTHOR: _____

_____

PLOT NOTES: _____

_____

_____

_____

_____

_____

_____

CHARACTER NOTES: _____

_____

_____

_____

_____

_____

FAVORITE QUOTES: _____

_____

_____

_____

_____

OTHER BOOKS TO READ BY THIS AUTHOR: _____

_____

DATE STARTED

___ / ___ / ___

DATE FINISHED

___ / ___ / ___

RATE THIS BOOK

1   2   3   4   5

, woe is me

T' have seen what I have seen,

see what I see!

OPHELIA

Hamlet by William Shakespeare

DATE STARTED

—— / —— / ——

DATE FINISHED

—— / —— / ——

RATE THIS BOOK

1   2   3   4   5

BOOK TITLE: _____

_____

AUTHOR: _____

_____

PLOT NOTES: _____

_____

_____

_____

_____

_____

_____

_____

CHARACTER NOTES: _____

_____

_____

_____

_____

_____

FAVORITE QUOTES: _____

_____

_____

_____

_____

_____

OTHER BOOKS TO READ BY THIS AUTHOR: _____

_____

BOOK TITLE: _____

_____

AUTHOR: _____

_____

PLOT NOTES: _____

_____

_____

_____

_____

_____

_____

CHARACTER NOTES: _____

_____

_____

_____

_____

_____

FAVORITE QUOTES: _____

_____

_____

_____

_____

_____

OTHER BOOKS TO READ BY THIS AUTHOR: _____

_____

DATE STARTED

___ / ___ / ___

DATE FINISHED

___ / ___ / ___

RATE THIS BOOK

1   2   3   4   5

DATE STARTED

___ / ___ / ___

DATE FINISHED

___ / ___ / ___

RATE THIS BOOK

1   2   3   4   5

BOOK TITLE: _____

_____

AUTHOR: _____

_____

PLOT NOTES: _____

_____

_____

_____

_____

_____

_____

_____

CHARACTER NOTES: _____

_____

_____

_____

_____

_____

_____

FAVORITE QUOTES: _____

_____

_____

_____

_____

_____

_____

OTHER BOOKS TO READ BY THIS AUTHOR: _____

_____

BOOK TITLE: _____

AUTHOR: _____

PLOT NOTES: _____
_____
_____
_____
_____
_____
_____

CHARACTER NOTES: _____
_____
_____
_____
_____
_____

FAVORITE QUOTES: _____
_____
_____
_____
_____
_____

OTHER BOOKS TO READ BY THIS AUTHOR: _____
_____

DATE STARTED

___ / ___ / ___

DATE FINISHED

___ / ___ / ___

RATE THIS BOOK

1   2   3   4   5

Thou must gather thine own sunshine.
I have none to give thee!

HESTER PRYNNE

The Scarlett Letter by Nathaniel Hawthorne

DATE STARTED

——— / ——— / ———

DATE FINISHED

——— / ——— / ———

RATE THIS BOOK

1   2   3   4   5

BOOK TITLE: _____

_____

AUTHOR: _____

_____

PLOT NOTES: _____

_____

_____

_____

_____

_____

_____

_____

CHARACTER NOTES: _____

_____

_____

_____

_____

_____

FAVORITE QUOTES: _____

_____

_____

_____

_____

_____

OTHER BOOKS TO READ BY THIS AUTHOR: _____

_____

BOOK TITLE: _____

_____

AUTHOR: _____

_____

PLOT NOTES: _____

_____

_____

_____

_____

_____

_____

CHARACTER NOTES: _____

_____

_____

_____

_____

_____

FAVORITE QUOTES: _____

_____

_____

_____

_____

_____

OTHER BOOKS TO READ BY THIS AUTHOR: _____

_____

DATE STARTED

___ / ___ / ___

DATE FINISHED

___ / ___ / ___

RATE THIS BOOK

1   2   3   4   5

DATE STARTED

___ / ___ / ___

DATE FINISHED

___ / ___ / ___

RATE THIS BOOK

1   2   3   4   5

BOOK TITLE: _____

_____

AUTHOR: _____

_____

PLOT NOTES: _____

_____

_____

_____

_____

_____

_____

CHARACTER NOTES: _____

_____

_____

_____

_____

_____

FAVORITE QUOTES: _____

_____

_____

_____

_____

_____

OTHER BOOKS TO READ BY THIS AUTHOR: _____

_____

BOOK TITLE: _____

_____

AUTHOR: _____

_____

PLOT NOTES: _____

_____

_____

_____

_____

_____

_____

_____

CHARACTER NOTES: _____

_____

_____

_____

_____

_____

FAVORITE QUOTES: _____

_____

_____

_____

_____

_____

OTHER BOOKS TO READ BY THIS AUTHOR: _____

_____

DATE STARTED

___ / ___ / ___

DATE FINISHED

___ / ___ / ___

RATE THIS BOOK

1 2 3 4 5

I wonder if I've been changed in the night?

Let me think: was I the same when I got up this morning?

I almost think I can remember feeling a little different.

But if I'm not the same, the next question is

"Who in the world am I?"

ALICE
Alice's Adventures in Wonderland by Lewis Carroll

DATE STARTED

—— / —— / ——

DATE FINISHED

—— / —— / ——

RATE THIS BOOK

1   2   3   4   5

BOOK TITLE: _____

_____

AUTHOR: _____

_____

PLOT NOTES: _____

_____

_____

_____

_____

_____

_____

CHARACTER NOTES: _____

_____

_____

_____

_____

_____

FAVORITE QUOTES: _____

_____

_____

_____

_____

_____

OTHER BOOKS TO READ BY THIS AUTHOR: _____

_____

BOOK TITLE: _____

DATE STARTED

___ / ___ / ___

AUTHOR: _____

DATE FINISHED

___ / ___ / ___

PLOT NOTES: _____

RATE THIS BOOK

1   2   3   4   5

CHARACTER NOTES: _____

FAVORITE QUOTES: _____

OTHER BOOKS TO READ BY THIS AUTHOR: _____

BOOKS TO CHECK OUT

BOOKS TO CHECK OUT

BOOK TITLE: _____

AUTHOR: _____

NOTES: _____

_____

_____

BOOK TITLE: _____

AUTHOR: _____

NOTES: _____

_____

_____

BOOK TITLE: _____

AUTHOR: _____

NOTES: _____

_____

_____

BOOK TITLE: _____

AUTHOR: _____

NOTES: _____

_____

_____

BOOKS TO CHECK OUT

BOOK TITLE: _____

AUTHOR: _____

NOTES: _____

_____

_____

BOOK TITLE: _____

AUTHOR: _____

NOTES: _____

_____

_____

BOOK TITLE: _____

AUTHOR: _____

NOTES: _____

_____

_____

BOOK TITLE: _____

AUTHOR: _____

NOTES: _____

_____

_____

Whatever our souls are made of,
his and mine are the same.

CATHERINE EARNSHAW

Wuthering Heights by Emily Brontë

BOOKS TO CHECK OUT

BOOK TITLE: _____

AUTHOR: _____

NOTES: _____

_____

_____

BOOK TITLE: _____

AUTHOR: _____

NOTES: _____

_____

_____

BOOK TITLE: _____

AUTHOR: _____

NOTES: _____

_____

_____

BOOK TITLE: _____

AUTHOR: _____

NOTES: _____

_____

_____

BOOKS TO CHECK OUT

BOOK TITLE: _____

AUTHOR: _____

NOTES: _____

_____

_____

_____

BOOK TITLE: _____

AUTHOR: _____

NOTES: _____

_____

_____

_____

BOOK TITLE: _____

AUTHOR: _____

NOTES: _____

_____

_____

_____

BOOK TITLE: _____

AUTHOR: _____

NOTES: _____

_____

_____

_____

BOOKS TO CHECK OUT

BOOK TITLE: _____

AUTHOR: _____

NOTES: _____

_____

_____

BOOK TITLE: _____

AUTHOR: _____

NOTES: _____

_____

_____

BOOK TITLE: _____

AUTHOR: _____

NOTES: _____

_____

_____

BOOK TITLE: _____

AUTHOR: _____

NOTES: _____

_____

_____

BOOKS TO CHECK OUT

BOOK TITLE: _____

AUTHOR: _____

NOTES: _____

_____

_____

_____

BOOK TITLE: _____

AUTHOR: _____

NOTES: _____

_____

_____

_____

BOOK TITLE: _____

AUTHOR: _____

NOTES: _____

_____

_____

_____

BOOK TITLE: _____

AUTHOR: _____

NOTES: _____

_____

_____

_____

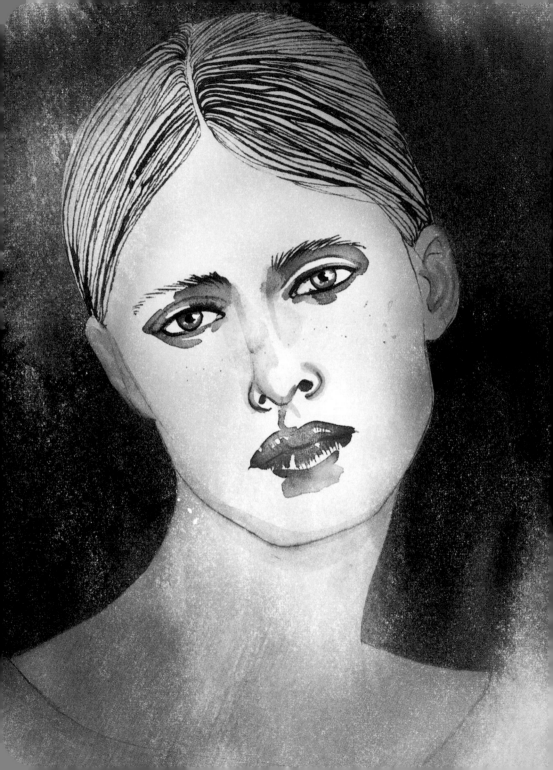

Oh, do not move!
do not speak!
look at me!
Something so sweet
comes from
your eyes
that helps me
so much!

EMMA BOVARY
Madame Bovary by Gustave Flaubert

BOOKS TO CHECK OUT

BOOK TITLE: _____

AUTHOR: _____

NOTES: _____

_____

_____

BOOK TITLE: _____

AUTHOR: _____

NOTES: _____

_____

_____

BOOK TITLE: _____

AUTHOR: _____

NOTES: _____

_____

_____

BOOK TITLE: _____

AUTHOR: _____

NOTES: _____

_____

_____

BOOKS TO CHECK OUT

BOOK TITLE: _____

AUTHOR: _____

NOTES: _____

_____

_____

_____

BOOK TITLE: _____

AUTHOR: _____

NOTES: _____

_____

_____

_____

BOOK TITLE: _____

AUTHOR: _____

NOTES: _____

_____

_____

_____

BOOK TITLE: _____

AUTHOR: _____

NOTES: _____

_____

_____

BOOKS TO CHECK OUT

BOOK TITLE: _____

AUTHOR: _____

NOTES: _____

_____

_____

BOOK TITLE: _____

AUTHOR: _____

NOTES: _____

_____

_____

BOOK TITLE: _____

AUTHOR: _____

NOTES: _____

_____

_____

BOOK TITLE: _____

AUTHOR: _____

NOTES: _____

_____

_____

BOOKS TO CHECK OUT

BOOK TITLE: _____

AUTHOR: _____

NOTES: _____

_____

_____

_____

BOOK TITLE: _____

AUTHOR: _____

NOTES: _____

_____

_____

_____

BOOK TITLE: _____

AUTHOR: _____

NOTES: _____

_____

_____

_____

BOOK TITLE: _____

AUTHOR: _____

NOTES: _____

_____

_____

NOTES, IDEAS, & OBSERVATIONS

NOTES / IDEAS / OBSERVATIONS

NOTES / IDEAS / OBSERVATIONS

NOTES / IDEAS / OBSERVATIONS

NOTES / IDEAS / OBSERVATIONS

I would give up the unessential;
    I would give my money,
I would give my life for my children;
    but I wouldn't give myself.

EDNA PONTELLIER
The Awakening by Kate Chopin

NOTES / IDEAS / OBSERVATIONS

NOTES / IDEAS / OBSERVATIONS

NOTES / IDEAS / OBSERVATIONS

NOTES / IDEAS / OBSERVATIONS

READING
INSPIRATION

READING INSPIRATION

The last page, the last line—how bittersweet it is to finish a book! Choosing your next read is the only salve. If you don't have a new book on deck, here's a sampling of winners of some of the major literary awards. These lists are by no means exhaustive, but perhaps your new favorite book will be among them.

NATIONAL BOOK AWARD FOR FICTION

The National Book Foundation rewards American writers (of many different genres, although here we cite only fiction) of exceptional merit. (www.nationalbook.org)

1950 *The Man with the Golden Arm*, Nelson Algren
1951 *The Collected Stories of William Faulkner*, William Faulkner
1952 *From Here to Eternity*, James Jones
1953 *Invisible Man*, Ralph Ellison
1954 *The Adventures of Augie March*, Saul Bellow
1955 *A Fable*, William Faulkner
1956 *Ten North Frederick*, John O'Hara
1957 *The Field of Vision*, Wright Morris
1958 *The Wapshot Chronicle*, John Cheever
1959 *The Magic Barrel*, Bernard Malamud
1960 *Goodbye, Columbus*, Philip Roth
1961 *The Waters of Kronos*, Conrad Richter
1962 *The Moviegoer*, Walker Percy
1963 *Morte D'Urban*, J. F. Powers
1964 *The Centaur*, John Updike
1965 *Herzog*, Saul Bellow
1966 *The Collected Stories of Katherine Anne Porter*, Katherine Anne Porter
1967 *The Fixer*, Bernard Malamud
1968 *The Eighth Day*, Thornton Wilder
1969 *Steps*, Jerzy Kosinski

1970 *Them,* Joyce Carol Oates

1971 *Mr. Sammler's Planet,* Saul Bellow

1972 *The Complete Stories,* Flannery O'Connor

1973 *Chimera,* John Barth, and *Augustus,* John Williams

1974 *Gravity's Rainbow,* Thomas Pynchon, and *A Crown of Feathers,* Isaac Bashevis Singer

1975 *Dog Soldiers,* Robert Stone, and *The Hair of Harold Roux,* Thomas Williams

1976 *JR,* William Gaddis

1977 *The Spectator Bird,* Wallace Stegner

1978 *Blood Tie,* Mary Lee Settle

1979 *Going After Cacciato,* Tim O'Brien

1980 *Sophie's Choice,* William Styron, and *The World According to Garp,* John Irving

1981 *Plains Song,* Wright Morris, and *The Stories of John Cheever,* John Cheever

1982 *Rabbit is Rich,* John Updike, and *So Long, See You Tomorrow,* William Maxwell

1983 *The Color Purple,* Alice Walker, and *The Collected Stories of Eudora Welty,* Eudora Welty

1984 *Victory Over Japan: A Book of Stories,* Ellen Gilchrist

1985 *White Noise,* Don DeLillo

1986 *World's Fair,* E. L. Doctorow

1987 *Paco's Story,* Larry Heinemann

1988 *Paris Trout,* Pete Dexter

1989 *Spartina,* John Casey

1990 *Middle Passage,* Charles Johnson

1991 *Mating,* Norman Rush

1992 *All the Pretty Horses,* Cormac McCarthy

1993 *The Shipping News,* E. Annie Proulx

1994 *A Frolic of His Own,* William Gaddis

1995 *Sabbath's Theater,* Philip Roth

1996 *Ship Fever and Other Stories,* Andrea Barrett

1997 *Cold Mountain,* Charles Frazier

1998 *Charming Billy,* Alice McDermott

1999 *Waiting,* Ha Jin

2000 *In America*, Susan Sontag
2001 *The Corrections*, Jonathan Franzen
2002 *Three Junes*, Julia Glass
2003 *The Great Fire*, Shirley Hazzard
2004 *The News from Paraguay*, Lily Tuck
2005 *Europe Central*, William T. Vollmann
2006 *The Echo Maker*, Richard Powers
2007 *Tree of Smoke*, Denis Johnson
2008 *Shadow Country*, Peter Matthiessen
2009 *Let the Great World Spin*, Colum McCann
2010 *Lord of Misrule*, Jaimy Gordon
2011 *Salvage the Bones*, Jesmyn Ward
2012 *The Round House*, Louise Erdrich
2013 *The Good Lord Bird*, James McBride

MAN BOOKER PRIZE

The Man Booker Prize is given to a full-length novel written by a citizen of the British Commonwealth or the Republic of Ireland. The novel must be an original work in English (not a translation) and must not be self-published. (www.themanbookerprize.com)

1969 *Something to Answer For*, P. H. Newby
1970 *The Elected Member*, Bernice Rubens
1971 *In a Free State*, V. S. Naipaul
1972 *G*, John Berger
1973 *The Seige of Krishnapur*, J. G. Farrell
1974 *The Conservationist*, Nadine Gordimer, and *Holiday*, Stanley Middleton
1975 *Heat and Dust*, Ruth Prawer Jhabvala
1976 *Saville*, David Storey
1977 *Staying On*, Paul Scott
1978 *The Sea, The Sea*, Iris Murdoch
1979 *Offshore*, Penelope Fitzgerald
1980 *Rites of Passage*, William Golding

1981 *Midnight's Children*, Salman Rushdie

1982 *Schindler's Ark*, Thomas Keneally

1983 *Life & Times of Michael K.*, J. M. Coetzee

1984 *Hotel du Lac*, Anita Brookner

1985 *The Bone People*, Keri Hulme

1986 *The Old Devils*, Kingsley Amis

1987 *Moon Tiger*, Penelope Lively

1988 *Oscar and Lucinda*, Peter Carey

1989 *The Remains of the Day*, Kazuo Ishiguro

1990 *Possession: A Romance*, A. S. Byatt

1991 *The Famished Road*, Ben Okri

1992 *The English Patient*, Michael Ondaatje, and *Sacred Hunger*, Barry Unsworth

1993 *Paddy Clarke Ha Ha Ha*, Roddy Doyle

1994 *How Late It Was, How Late*, James Kelman

1995 *The Ghost Road*, Pat Barker

1996 *Last Orders*, Graham Swift

1997 *The God of Small Things*, Arundhati Roy

1998 *Amsterdam*, Ian McEwan

1999 *Disgrace*, J. M. Coetzee

2000 *The Blind Assassin*, Margaret Atwood

2001 *True History of the Kelly Gang*, Peter Carey

2002 *Life of Pi*, Yann Martel

2003 *Vernon God Little*, DBC Pierre

2004 *The Line of Beauty*, Alan Hollinghurst

2005 *The Sea*, John Banville

2006 *The Inheritance of Loss*, Kiran Desai

2007 *The Gathering*, Anne Enright

2008 *The White Tiger*, Aravind Adiga

2009 *Wolf Hall*, Hilary Mantel

2010 *The Finkler Question*, Howard Jacobson

2011 *The Sense of an Ending*, Julian Barnes

2012 *Bring Up the Bodies*, Hilary Mantel

2013 *The Luminaries*, Eleanor Catton

PEN/FAULKNER AWARD FOR FICTION

The PEN/Faulkner Award for Fiction is awarded to living American fiction writers. (www.penfaulkner.org)

1981 *How German Is It*, Walter Abish
1982 *The Chaneysville Incident*, David Bradley
1983 *Seaview*, Toby Olson
1984 *Sent for You Yesterday*, John Edgar Wideman
1985 *The Barracks Thief*, Tobias Wolff
1986 *The Old Forest and Other Stories*, Peter Taylor
1987 *Soldiers in Hiding*, Richard Wiley
1988 *World's End*, T. Coraghessan Boyle
1989 *Dusk and Other Stories*, James Salter
1990 *Billy Bathgate*, E. L. Doctorow
1991 *Philadelphia Fire*, John Edgar Wideman
1992 *Mao II*, Don DeLillo
1993 *Postcards*, E. Annie Proulx
1994 *Operation Shylock*, Philip Roth
1995 *Snow Falling on Cedars*, David Guterson
1996 *Independence Day*, Richard Ford
1997 *Women in Their Beds*, Gina Berriault
1998 *The Bear Comes Home*, Rafi Zabor
1999 *The Hours*, Michael Cunningham
2000 *Waiting*, Ha Jin
2001 *The Human Stain*, Philip Roth
2002 *Bel Canto*, Ann Patchett
2003 *The Caprices*, Sabina Murray
2004 *The Early Stories: 1953–1975*, John Updike
2005 *War Trash*, Ha Jin
2006 *The March*, E. L. Doctorow
2007 *Everyman*, Philip Roth
2008 *The Great Man*, Kate Christensen
2009 *Netherland*, Joseph O'Neill
2010 *War Dances*, Sherman Alexie
2011 *The Collected Stories of Deborah Eisenberg*, Deborah Eisenberg

2012 *The Buddha in the Attic,* Julie Otsuka
2013 *Everything Begins & Ends at the Kentucky Club,* Benjamin Alire Sáenz
2014 *We Are All Completely Beside Ourselves,* Karen Joy Fowler

PULITZER PRIZE FOR FICTION

The Pulitzer Prizes are awarded in many different categories, most famously for journalism. The Pulitzer for fiction is awarded for "distinguished fiction by an American author, preferably dealing with American life." No Pulitzer prizes for fiction were awarded for the years 1954, 1957, 1964, 1971, 1974, 1977, and 2012. (www.pulitzer.org)

1948 *Tales of the South Pacific,* James A. Michener
1949 *Guard of Honor,* James Gould Cozzens
1950 *The Way West,* A. B. Guthrie, Jr.
1951 *The Town,* Conrad Richter
1952 *The Caine Mutiny,* Herman Wouk
1953 *The Old Man and the Sea,* Ernest Hemingway
1955 *A Fable,* William Faulkner
1956 *Andersonville,* MacKinlay Kantor
1958 *A Death in the Family,* James Agee
1959 *The Travels of Jaimie McPheeters,* Robert Lewis Taylor
1960 *Advise and Consent,* Allen Drury
1961 *To Kill a Mockingbird,* Harper Lee
1962 *The Edge of Sadness,* Edwin O'Connor
1963 *The Reivers,* William Faulkner
1965 *The Keepers of the House,* Shirley Ann Grau
1966 *The Collected Stories of Katherine Anne Porter,* Katherine Anne Porter
1967 *The Fixer,* Bernard Malamud
1968 *The Confessions of Nat Turner,* William Styron
1969 *House Made of Dawn,* N. Scott Momaday
1970 *The Collected Stories of Jean Stafford,* Jean Stafford
1972 *Angle of Repose,* Wallace Stegner
1973 *The Optimist's Daughter,* Eudora Welty
1975 *The Killer Angels,* Michael Shaara
1976 *Humboldt's Gift,* Saul Bellow

1978 *Elbow Room*, James Alan McPherson
1979 *The Stories of John Cheever*, John Cheever
1980 *The Executioner's Song*, Norman Mailer
1981 *A Confederacy of Dunces*, John Kennedy Toole
1982 *Rabbit Is Rich*, John Updike
1983 *The Color Purple*, Alice Walker
1984 *Ironweed*, William Kennedy
1985 *Foreign Affairs*, Alison Lurie
1986 *Lonesome Dove*, Larry McMurtry
1987 *A Summons to Memphis*, Peter Taylor
1988 *Beloved*, Toni Morrison
1989 *Breathing Lessons*, Anne Tyler
1990 *The Mambo Kings Play Songs of Love*, Oscar Hijuelos
1991 *Rabbit at Rest*, John Updike
1992 *A Thousand Acres*, Jane Smiley
1993 *A Good Scent from a Strange Mountain*, Robert Olen Butler
1994 *The Shipping News*, E. Annie Proulx
1995 *The Stone Diaries*, Carol Shields
1996 *Independence Day*, Richard Ford
1997 *Martin Dressler: The Tale of an American Dreamer*, by Steven Millhauser
1998 *American Pastoral*, Philip Roth
1999 *The Hours*, Michael Cunningham
2000 *Interpreter of Maladies*, Jhumpa Lahiri
2001 *The Amazing Adventures of Kavalier & Clay*, Michael Chabon
2002 *Empire Falls*, Richard Russo
2003 *Middlesex*, Jeffrey Eugenides
2004 *The Known World*, Edward P. Jones
2005 *Gilead*, Marilynne Robinson
2006 *March*, Geraldine Brooks
2007 *The Road*, Cormac McCarthy
2008 *The Brief Wondrous Life of Oscar Wao*, Junot Díaz
2009 *Olive Kitteridge*, Elizabeth Strout
2010 *Tinkers*, Paul Harding
2011 *A Visit from the Goon Squad*, Jennifer Egan
2013 *The Orphan Master's Son*, Adam Johnson
2014 *The Goldfinch*, Donna Tartt

MY PRIZEWINNERS

What books would you award highest honors?

_____

BOOK TITLE: _____

AUTHOR: _____

DATE READ: _____

_____

BOOK TITLE: _____

AUTHOR: _____

DATE READ: _____

_____

BOOK TITLE: _____

AUTHOR: _____

DATE READ: _____

_____

BOOK TITLE: _____

AUTHOR: _____

DATE READ: _____

_____

BOOK TITLE: _____

AUTHOR: _____

DATE READ: _____

_____

BOOK TITLE: _____

AUTHOR: _____

DATE READ: _____

BOOK TITLE: _____

AUTHOR: _____

DATE READ: _____

BOOK TITLE: _____

AUTHOR: _____

DATE READ: _____

BOOK TITLE: _____

AUTHOR: _____

DATE READ: _____

BOOK TITLE: _____

AUTHOR: _____

DATE READ: _____

BOOK TITLE: _____

AUTHOR: _____

DATE READ: _____

BOOK TITLE: _____

AUTHOR: _____

DATE READ: _____

BOOK TITLE: _____

AUTHOR: _____

DATE READ: _____

BOOK TITLE: _____

AUTHOR: _____

DATE READ: _____

BOOK TITLE: _____

AUTHOR: _____

DATE READ: _____

BOOK TITLE: _____

AUTHOR: _____

DATE READ: _____

BOOK TITLE: _____

AUTHOR: _____

DATE READ: _____

isn't it nice to think

that tomorrow is a new day
with no mistakes in it yet?

ANNE SHIRLEY

Anne of Green Gables by Lucy Maud Montgomery